Songwriting

for beginners

Alfred, the leader in educational publishing,
and the National Guitar Workshop,
one of America's finest guitar schools, have joined
forces to bring you the best, most progressive
educational tools possible. We hope you will enjoy
this book and encourage you to look for
other fine products from Alfred and the
National Guitar Workshop.

An Easy Beginning Method

Time and dis-tance seem to dis-ap-pear,

MIRIAM DAVIDSON & KIYA HEARTWOOD

Acquisition, editorial, typesetting and internal design: Nathaniel Gunod, Workshop Arts
Consulting editors: Ron Manus and Link Harnsberger, Alfred Publishing
Art Direction: Ted Engelbart • Cover design/illustration: Martha Widmann
Piano materials for cover artwork provided by: International Piano Supply,
Piano Accessories • http://www.pianosupply.com • ips@pianosupply.com • 818-366-3761
Guitar materials for cover artwork provided by: Will Ray of the Hellicasters

2

Contents

About the Authors

Miriam Davidson (left) is a singer, songwriter, instrumentalist and international recording artist. She has been teaching at the National Guitar Summer Workshop since its inception in 1984, where she heads the Voice and Songwriting departments. She is a member of the Terrakin recording group, Wishing Chair, which she founded with Kiya Heartwood.

Kiya Heartwood (right) is an internationally known recording artist and songwriter. She was the founding member and songwriter of Stealin' Horses, Arista recording artists. She has written and recorded seven albums, which include a top 40 AOR hit, *Turnaround*, and a Number 1 independent country hit, *Home*. Kiya has performed her songs throughout the United States and Canada. She is a teacher of songwriting at the National Guitar Summer Workshop.

Wishing Chair's latest recording, *Singing With the Red Wolves*, is available from Terrakin Records.

Introduction

Everyone, at one time or another, has probably wanted to write a song, whether for a school play, a local band or a parody at a birthday party. No matter what kind of song you write, the tools you need are basically the same. At its most simple, an idea for a story and a melody and some knowledge about how to fit them together are all you need.

There is no best way to write a song. Writing a song is very much like fitting pieces of a puzzle together: once you get going with an idea, it's a matter of laying your pieces out on the table and then getting them to fit. This book is designed to provide you with all the tools you will need to write a well crafted song.

You don't really need to have any previous experience to write songs. Just the desire is necessary. You don't even have to play an instrument. Many songwriters don't know how to read music. However, the more you do know, the easier it will be for you write. This book starts you at the very beginning and takes you step by step through the songwriting process. It will explain the basics of music theory, show you simple chords on the guitar and keyboard, tell you how to write lyrics and melodies, and how to put chord progressions together.

Writing a song can be approached from any direction. You can begin with an idea for a melody, a story you wish to tell or a poem that you think could make a good song. As your ideas begin to form and the song takes shape, you may find that it is coming out in a way that you hadn't planned. This is good. It means that you are letting yourself go and listening to that creative spark inside. There will be plenty of time to look at it critically and make adjustments.

While it is not necessary to go through the book in order, you will find that following a step by step approach is a very good way to start. Once you understand all the elements of songwriting you will find it easier to write from many different viewpoints.

Each of us has our own unique way of approaching the creative process. Some people have a specific time that they set aside for writing and do it no matter what. A lot of us get inspired by some spark which starts us off — a thought we had while driving, little bits of a melody, or a chord progression we were fiddling around with. The more you write, the more you will find yourself being inspired by many different sources. As in all things, practice is very important. Complete the suggested exercises throughout the book, and you will be well on your way to successful songwriting. Have fun and good luck!

Chapter 1

The Basics

What Is a Song?

A song is made up of words and music woven together in a way that is satisfying and complete in the eyes and ears of the songwriter. Hopefully, it is also satisfying to the listener. A song is, in many ways, like a house. A house needs a strong foundation or it won't stand. You can build it out of many elements. It doesn't really matter if the house is built of brick or wood as long as, in the end, all the pieces work together. A song is built from many components — a melody, a strong, catchy phrase, a story the writer wishes to tell. Any of these can act as its foundation. It doesn't matter which of these elements the songwriter chooses to use as long as they all feel like they belong together.

The two main parts of a song are the *music* and the *lyrics*. The music sets the mood and communicates the emotions the writer is trying to express without anyone ever uttering a word. The lyrics tell the story and take the listener where the writer wants them to go.

The music is made up of three parts: the *melody* (the tune that the lyrics follow), the *harmony* (sounds that are played or sung with the melody), and the *rhythm* (the beat) that holds all this in place. Music expresses emotions and sets the mood of the song before any words are used. In this respect, the songwriter has a great advantage over the writer or poet as they have this extra tool, music, at their disposal to help convey their ideas.

The lyrics are the words of the song. They should sound like they fit together with the music. For example, a sad love song would not have a foot-tapping, happy tune.

The writing of a song can be approached from many directions — the lyrics first, the music first or both simultaneously — as long as the finished product seems like all its parts work together. If it is done well, you won't notice the seams between its sections. The song should flow and feel like it was all written at once. The more ways you know how to write a song, the easier it will become to find the perfect approach for each new idea.

> *Exercise*
> Listen to your favorite CD and try to separate out the melody, harmony, rhythm and lyrics for each song. This will help you begin to develop a critical ear.

Song Elements

Every song is comprised of a pattern of elements that holds the song together in one solid form. This structure can be divided into sections:

1. Verse
2. Chorus
3. Bridge
4. Hook
5. Refrain

All songs are put together with some or all of these parts in a particular pattern. These patterns are familiar to the listener and create a comfortable design in which to express your ideas. Common patterns have evolved over time and are easily recognizable. One such pattern is the *verse/chorus* format.

For instance, the chorus in the popular Christmas song, *Jingle Bells*, by J. Pierpont, consists of these familiar words:

> *chorus:* *Jingle bells, jingle bells,*
> *Jingle all the way.*
> *Oh what fun it is to ride*
> *in a one horse open sleigh, Hey!*

Then comes the verse, or story:

> *verse:* *Dashing through the snow*
> *In a one horse open sleigh*
> *O'er the fields we go*
> *Laughing all the way.*
> *Bells on bob-tail ring*
> *Making spirits bright*
> *What fun it is to ride and sing*
> *A sleighing song tonight. Oh,*

In this song the verse and the chorus alternate from one to the other as the story progresses. It is the familiarity of patterns such as this that draws the listener in and makes them receptive to what you are trying to say. A writer who understands this principle can also surprise the listener and make something new and interesting happen by deviating from what is expected. In other words, it pays to know the rules in order to break them effectively.

VERSE
The verse contains the details of the song: the story, the events, images and emotions that the writer wishes to express. A verse will be more specific and detailed than the chorus. Each verse will have different lyrics than the others. It should move the story toward its logical conclusion. Musically, the melody and chord pattern will stay uniform, or vary only slightly to keep the listener's attention on the message of the words. The rhyme pattern will also remain uniform, or vary only slightly. For example, *Waterfall* by TLC or *Piano Man* by Billy Joel are songs where this kind of slight variation is used.

CHORUS
The chorus is the part that everybody wants to sing along to. It is the section of the song that is easily remembered after the first hearing. The chorus contains the main idea, or big picture, of what is being expressed both lyrically and musically. It is repeated throughout the song, and the melody and lyric rarely vary. A great chorus is usually simple and easy to remember. Many times, the chorus is taken from the title of the song. If you can't recall the chorus after one or two hearings, chances are it's too wordy or clumsy. The secret of a successful chorus is contained in the old adage, K.I.S.S. (Keep It Simple, Stupid).

You don't need to talk down to your listeners. Try to say everything as straightforward and simply as possible. When you hear the chorus, you should know what the song is about. Good examples of this are *This Land is Your Land* by Woody Guthrie, *Down at the Twist and Shout* by Mary-Chapin Carpenter, and *Those Were the Days* by Gene Raskin.

HOOK

The *hook* is a phrase or a word that literally hooks, or grabs, the listener and draws them into the song. The hook is often in the chorus or refrain (see below). A hook may take a standard phrase or cliché and look at it from a fresh angle or alter it slightly to reveal a new and different meaning. A hook is absolutely essential to a successful song, especially a commercial one. The hook can be musical, such as a repeated guitar or keyboard riff. Think for a moment of the opening guitar line in the Beatles song, *Day Tripper*. It is instantly recognizable and would never be mistaken for another song. Or, how about Michael Jackson's song *Beat It*. Many hit songs have both a musical and lyrical hook. Take, for example, Janis Ian's *At Seventeen* or Willie Nelson's *Crazy*. If you know the old folk song, *Pop Goes the Weasel*, you are well acquainted with the idea of a hook. Just think of the tune to the words "Pop goes the weasel." That's a hook!

BRIDGE

The *bridge* is a device that is used to break up the repetitive pattern of a song and keep the listeners attention. It often appears after the chorus, but this is not a rule written in stone. In a bridge, the pattern of the words and the music change. Many songs have instrumental/musical bridges. *The Tracks of My Tears* by Smokey Robinson and *Greatest Love of All* by Linda Creed are two great examples of songs with bridges. Not every song has a bridge. A song without a bridge would be *You Are the Sunshine of My Life* by Stevie Wonder. An experienced writer will develop a feel for when a bridge is useful or necessary. Think of the song *Country Roads* by John Denver: the part where the lyrics talk about being reminded of a far away home is the bridge. Listen to this great song—you'll notice that the melody in this part is very different from the rest of the song. This distinguishes it as the bridge.

REFRAIN

A repeated line or musical phrase that ties a song together is known as a *refrain*. This is a common element in many musical styles, such as rap or traditional folk songs. A refrain acts as the chorus. It works like a chorus in that it is unchanging and often repeated. A refrain is only a phrase, or a word, while a chorus contains many more words. Good examples of songs with a refrain are *You Shook Me All Night Long* by AC/DC or *Sounds of Silence* by Paul Simon. Think of the popular Christmas song, *Deck the Halls*. The phrase with the words "Fa la la la la, la la la la" is a refrain.

> *Exercise*
> Turn on the radio and listen to three different kinds of stations; country, alternative and oldies. Pick three songs from each, and identify all of these elements: verse, chorus, hook, bridge and refrain.

Common Song Forms

A song's structure can be described using capital letters to represent each element. This shorthand can serve as a blueprint of the song's form, and makes it easier for us to understand what we are doing. The first section is represented by the letter "A," the next complete section by the letter "B" and the next by the letter "C." When a section repeats, we show the letter twice. For instance, two verses in a row would be written A - A. There are many common patterns. Let's discuss the three that are most commonly used.

A - A - A

Here, there is no variety in the melody or lyric pattern. This is a form followed by many older folk songs and ballads. Bob Dylan followed this pattern many times in his early songs. For example, *The Times They Are a Changin'* and follows this format. *House of the Rising Sun*, as sung by the Animals, is another great example. The old folk song *Clementine* also follows this pattern. The music for the verses stays the same as the story progresses. *Runaround* and *Hook*, both by Blues Traveler, are more good examples of this form.

A - B - A

This simple verse/chorus or chorus/verse pattern is used in many styles of music. An example of the chorus-first pattern is *Turn, Turn Turn* by Pete Seeger. The Byrds made this song a number #1 hit. From a Distance by Julie Gold. A verse-first example is *Honky Tonk Woman* by the Rolling Stones. Sometimes this pattern is two verses followed by a chorus, which is common in contemporary country music. *American Honky Tonk Bar Association* by Brian Kennedy and Jim Rushing is an example of this pattern.

A - B - A - B - C - B

This variation is a common one, especially in pop music. It adds a bridge to the verse/chorus pattern. Many Motown songs are classic examples of this form, such as *My Guy* by Smokey Robinson. Can't Hurry Love redone by Phil Collins. The Beatles song *Ticket to Ride* also follows this pattern.

No matter what blueprint you decide to follow, the best tools are your own ears. If you feel the song is missing something, try varying or altering the pattern. Ultimately a song is right when you are happy with it. Remember, you are the first listener.

Exercise

From your favorite album, pick five songs and analyze the structure of each. Pick three songs from different styles of music and analyze them as well.

Chapter 2

Writing Music

The musical part of your song, as mentioned earlier, can be broken up into three basic parts:

1. *Melody* - the tune that you sing with the lyrics.
2. *Harmony* - the music that is played or sung with the melody.
3. *Rhythm* - the beat that holds everything in place.

Which of these you write first is entirely up to you. You may be the kind of person who gets a melody line in your head and then adds harmony to it. Or you may hear a beat in your head first and then think of a melody line to go with it. In either case, the more you understand about music and music theory the better off you will be. Don't let the word "theory" scare you. Understanding the basics of how music works is a simple process. Let's go through it one small step at a time.

THE MUSICAL ALPHABET

Every musical sound or note has a name which is taken from the letters of the alphabet. The musical alphabet has only seven letters: A ,B, C, D, E, F and G. These letters repeat themselves over and over:

A   B   C   D   E   F   G   A   B   C   D   etc.

The distance between two notes with the same name is called an *octave*. They are the same note but one will sound higher or lower than the other.

The distance from one note to another in the musical alphabet is measured in steps. Steps come in two sizes: *half steps* and *whole steps*. Let's see what half steps and whole steps look like on a keyboard.

Half step:
The distance from any key to an adjacent key, black or white. For example, from the first white key to the next black key is one half step. Or: the distance from a white key to the next white key not separated by a black key.

Half step

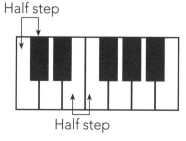

Half step

Whole step:
The distance of two half steps. For example, from the first white key to the next white key is a whole step. Or, if there is no black key between two white keys, from a white key to the next higher black key is a whole step.

Whole step

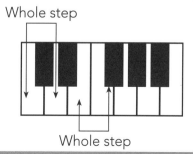

Whole step

Here is what half steps and whole steps look like on a guitar fingerboard:

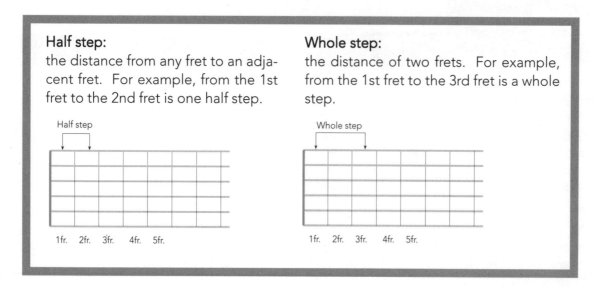

The notes of the musical alphabet (sometimes called *natural notes*) have the following arrangement of half steps and whole steps:

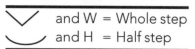

Finding the natural notes on the keyboard is an easy process. The natural notes fall on the white keys and follow each other in a line. Notice how a note will appear in the same place in relation to the black keys no matter where you are on the keyboard.

If you know the names of the open strings of the guitar you can use your knowledge of half steps and whole steps to find the natural notes on the guitar fingerboard.

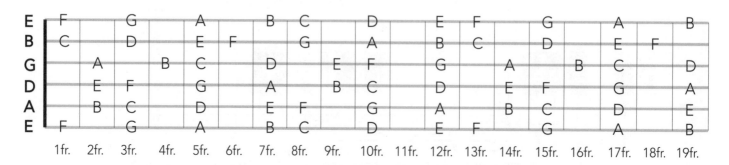

Reading Music—Pitch

Notes
Pitch refers to the highness or lowness of musical sounds, called notes. Pitch is indicated by placing *notes* on a staff. Some notes have *stems* while others do not.

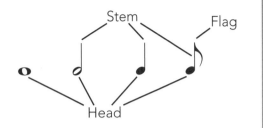

The Staff and Clef
The *staff* has five lines and four spaces. It is read from left to right. The symbol at the beginning of the staff is a *clef*. The clef tells us what notes correspond to a particular line or space on the staff. The ending curl of the *treble clef* (shown here) encircles the G line and is sometimes called a *G clef*.

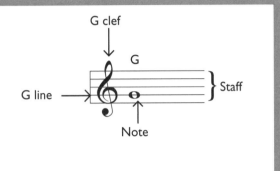

An easy way to begin reading music is to memorize the names of the lines and spaces. The higher or lower a note is written on the staff, the higher or lower is actually sounds. There are five line notes and four space notes. Notes above and below the staff have *ledger lines*. Notes on ledger lines are easy to read because they look different form the others.

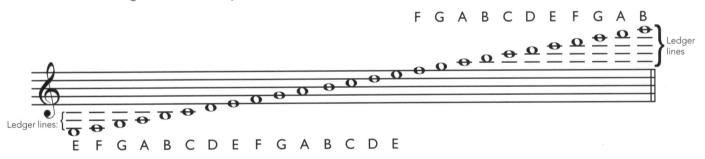

Piano players must be able to read *bass clef*, or *F clef* 𝄢. Generally, the left hand part is appears in F clef. The principle is the same as for the G clef. In this case however, the clef indicates which line will be "F." The examples below show how you can use phrases and words to help remember the names of the notes on the staff in each clef.

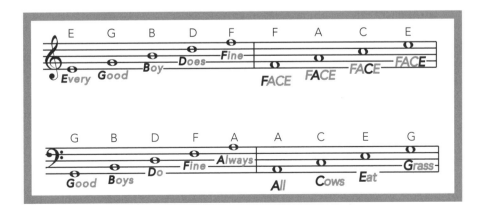

Reading Music — Time

Measures

Measures divide music into groups of *beats*. A beat is an equal division of time. Beats are the basic pulse behind music. The vertical lines that cross through the staff are called *bar lines*. They show where one measure ends and another begins. *Double bars* mark the end of a section or the end of a song.

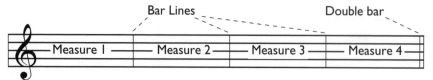

Note Durations

As you know, the location of a note on the staff tells us its pitch (how high or low). Its duration, or value, is indicated by its shape.

Whole note	Half notes	Quarter notes	Eighth notes	Sixteenth notes
4 beats	2 beats each	1 beat each	½ beat each	¼ beat each

Rests

So far we've talked about five types of note values. They each have a corresponding period of silence known as a *rest*. A whole rest means four beats of silence, a half rest means two beats of silence, and so on.

Whole note rest	Half note rest	Quarter note rest	Eighth note rest	Sixteenth note rest
4 beats	2 beats	1 beat	½ beat	¼ beat

Time Signatures

At the beginning of any piece of music you will find the *time signature*. A time signature consists of two numbers, one above the other, which looks like a fraction. The top number tells us how many beats are in each measure. The bottom number tells us what kind of note gets one count.

$\dfrac{4}{4}$ ← 4 beats per measure
← Quarter note ♩ = 1 beat

$\dfrac{3}{4}$ ← 3 beats per measure
← Quarter note ♩ = 1 beat

The time signature you will come across most often is $\frac{4}{4}$. For this reason it is often called *common time* and is indicated by a **C**.

The Major Scale

A *scale* is a group of notes that follow each other in a pattern of half steps and whole steps. While there are many different and unusual scales, the most useful to us right now is the *major scale*. The following diagram shows how whole and half steps create a pattern which we recognize as the major scale.

C Major Scale

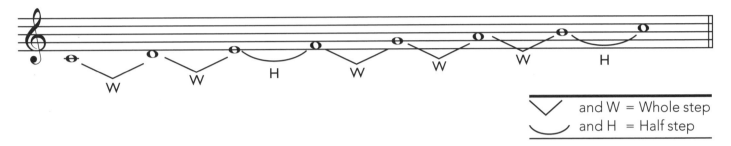

A scale is named after its *root* (first) note. For example, the C Major scale begins on the note C. To build a major scale on any note other than C, we will have to raise or lower the natural notes to make them fit the scale formula. We do this with *accidentals*.

Accidentals

An accidental is a symbol that alters the pitch of a note.

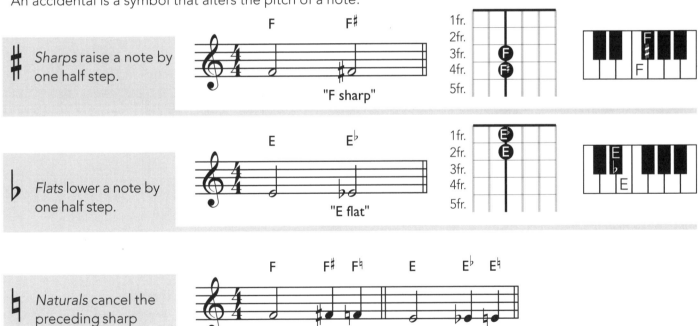

Here is how accidentals, in this case, sharps, would be applied to create a major scale starting on A.

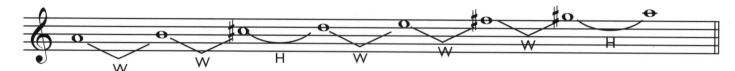

We assign a number to each of the notes in the scale. This shows each note's particular place in the scale. For instance, in the A Major scale above, A=1, B=2, C#=3 and so on. Since the 8th note in the scale is the same as the 1st, it is often called "1."

Chords

A *chord* contains three or more notes. To each note of the major scale we add two more notes in order to build a chord. We add these notes using *intervals*. An interval is the distance from one note to another inclusively. For example, C to D is the interval of a 2nd (C_1, D_2). C to E is the interval of a 3rd (C_1, D_2, E_3). The lowest note of the chord is the *root*, of that chord, and is the note that the chord is named after. When we add the note that is an interval of a third above the root we get the next note in the chord. The note which is a third above that gives us the next note.

Here is how we would build a C Major chord, or *triad*. Triad refers to a chord containing three pitches.

Major

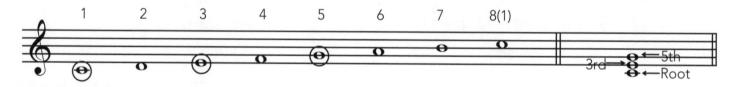

We refer to the notes of the major chord as the *Root*, *3rd* and *5th*. For instance, in a C Major chord, C is the root. The E is the 3rd (3) because it is an interval (distance) of a 3rd from the root. The G is the 5th (5) because it is an interval of a 5th from the root.

We assign a number to each chord built from a particular scale, shown by a Roman numeral. This shows each note's particular place in the scale. For instance, the C Major triad above would be called "I" because it is built on the 1st note in the scale. In case it has been a while since your last encounter with Roman numerals, you can refer to the chart below to refresh your memory. Both upper and lower case forms are shown.

I	i	1	IV	iv	4	VII	vii	7	X	x	10
II	ii	2	V	v	5	VIII	viii	8	XI	xi	11
III	iii	3	VI	vi	6	IX	ix	9	XII	xii	12

We can build a triad on each note of a major scale, which will give us all the chords available in that particular major key. Because of the position of the whole steps and half steps in the major scale, each of these chords has a particular sound or quality. Having seen the formula for the major triad on page 14, let's look at the other triad types.

Minor
If we lower, or flat, the 3rd scale degree of a major chord (3 becomes ♭3) we get a *minor* chord. We can abbreviate the word minor by writing *min* or lowercase *m*.

Diminished
If we take that minor chord and flat the 5th scale degree (5 becomes ♭5) we get a *diminished* chord. We can abbreviate the word diminished by writing *dim* or a small circle (o).

The Chords of the Major Scale
Now we will build triads on all the scale tones of the C Major scale. Upper case Roman numerals indicate a major chord while lower case indicates a minor or diminished chord.

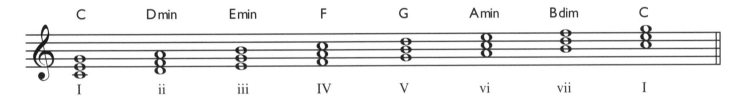

If we stack another 3rd above our 5th (adding a 7th above the root of each chord) we get what are known as 7th chords. This one note adds a lot of texture and gives each chord a richer sound. These chords tend to have a jazzier feel and are used extensively in blues, rock and jazz songs.

Here is what the C Major scale now looks like with 7th chords.

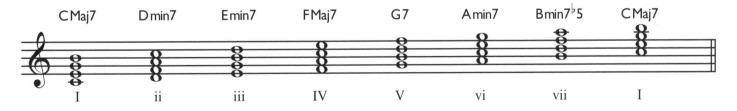

> We now have what are known as *diatonic* 7th chords.
> Diatonic means "belonging to the scale."

There are several different kinds of 7th chords and they each have a particular sound or quality:

name	abbreviation
Major 7th	(Maj7)
Dominant 7th	(dom7 or 7)
Minor 7th	(min7)
Minor 7th ♭5th	(min7♭5)
Diminished 7th	(dim7 or °)

The **major 7** chord, written Maj7, is built by adding a 3rd above the 5th of a I or IV chord. The 5th of a C Major chord (I) is the note G. Add a 3rd above the 5th and you get the note B.

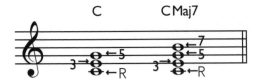

To build a **dominant 7** chord, written by adding a 7 after the root name (for example G7), add a 3rd on top of a V chord. The distance from this note to the root is a ♭7.

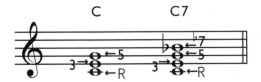

To make a **minor 7** chord, written min7, you add a minor 3rd to a minor triad (ii, iii or vi). The distance from this note to the root is a ♭7.

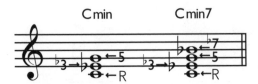

To build a **minor 7♭5** chord, written min7♭5, you add a 3rd above the 5th of a diminished triad (vii). The distance from this note to the root is a ♭7.

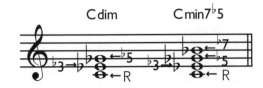

A **diminished 7** chord, written dim7 or °, adds a ♭3 above the 5th of a diminished triad (vii). The distance from this note to the root is a diminished 7th (count up a 7th from the root and lower the note by two half steps).

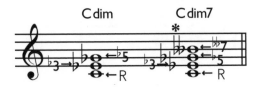

The best thing about diatonic 7th chords is that their qualities remain the same no matter what key you are in. In other words, I and IV are always major 7th chords, ii, iii and vi are always minor 7th chords, and vii is always a minor 7♭5. In any given key we now have a rich palette of sounds from which to create our harmonies.

* ♭♭ = double flat. This means to

Chord Progressions

How do you know which chords to use? To construct a *chord progression* (sequence of chords) you must decide what chords to put together to complement your melody (if you have one). Remember that each chord has its own particular sound or mood. So, if you already have the lyrics or know what kind of mood you wish to create, your chord choices will help bring out your song's colors and emotions. Of all the chords previously mentioned, those most commonly used in progressions are the I chord, the IV chord and the V chord. This is true for music of all styles. These three chords are the fundamental primary harmonies. The I chord, being built upon the root of the scale, gives us a feeling of stability, or rest. For that reason we often begin and end progressions with this chord. All the other chords supply movement or tension. So, as we move through a progression, we start at the beginning, I, go through some interesting territory, and then come back home, or *resolve*, to the I chord.

There are many ways to build upon this concept. Some chords have a natural tendency to move to certain other chords. It's what you might call a natural law of music. Think of it this way; just like there are three primary colors, red, yellow and blue, there are three *primary chords*, the I, the IV and the V. The I chord is called the *tonic*, the IV chord is called *subdominant*, and the V chord is called the *dominant*. We can mix our primary colors together to get other colors; red and yellow to get orange, yellow and blue to get green, red and blue to get purple. Each of those secondary colors feel closer in kinship to certain primary colors over other colors. Our *secondary chords*, the ii, iii, vi and vii, have notes in common with our primary chords. For this reason, we can use them to substitute for each other. Look at the example below. In each of the primary chord groups, you can see how the secondary chords share notes. This makes them sound similar but not quite the same.

CHORD SUBSTITUTIONS

The Basic Progression (I-IV-V-I)
Some chords sound like they naturally want to go to other chords. The V likes to go to the I, and the I likes to go to the IV. This is what makes I-IV-V-I work as the basic progression. Then, other chords from each group can be substituted.

I	IV	V	I	
C	F	G	C	or

I	IV	V	vi	
C	F	G	Amin	or

I	ii	V	vi	
C	Dmin	G	Amin	or

I	ii7	V7	I	
C	Dmin7	G7	C	etc.

> *Exercise*
>
> Play through each of these progressions and listen for the changes in the chord substitutions. Then, try creating your own progression using substitutions.

Here are some examples of commonly used chord progressions in the key of C:

1. I   IV   V   I
C   F   G   C

2. ii   V   I
Dmin   G   C

3. I   vi   IV   V   I
C   Amin F   G   C

4. I   ii   iii   ii   I
C   Dmin Emin Dmin C

There are also a few rules of thumb about what chords tend to go naturally with other chords. So if you find yourself fishing around for where to go to next, try using these suggestions.

I   - goes to any chord
ii - goes to iii, V or I
iii - goes to IV or vi
IV - goes to V, I, ii or iii
V - goes to I, IV or vi
vi - goes to I, iii or IV
vii - goes to vi or I

As you look at different progressions you will find that certain ones are used over and over. Look at the following example from several songs, in different styles, that all use basically the same chord progression (you may recognize this as the *Heart and Soul* progression):

I vi IV V

Blue Moon — Rogers/Hart
Hang On Sloopy — Russell/Farrell
Brown Eyed Girl — Van Morrison
If I Had a Hammer — Pete Seeger
I Will Always Love You — Dolly Parton
Just to See Her — Smokey Robinson

PHOTO • COURTESY OF MOTOWN

Smokey Robinson
A master craftsman, performer and songwriter, Smokey Robinson has been writing songs for over twenty-five years.

If you think that basic chord progressions are boring, remember that the key to a successful song is to set up a pattern that is comfortable for the listener. Then you can change a few small things so that the song remains interesting. If you're overcome with the urge to radically change things, try not to spice things up too much by coming up with something really unusual. Chances are good that it will be very hard to follow.

So, how do we get some contrast and interest in a progression without going out on too much of a limb?

We can change the quality of our chords (major to minor or minor to major), or go up or down by a half step (♭vii instead of vii or ♭iii instead of iii). By doing this we are going outside of the key, and using chords which are not natural to our diatonic progressions. This is a very cool and simple thing to do. Lennon and McCartney did it all the time. For example, in the key of C we could change the ii chord to II (D minor to D Major), the iii chord to III (E minor to E Major), the IV chord to iv (F Major to F minor) or the vi chord (A minor to A Major). The most effective place to do something like this is when you want to call attention to an important place in the lyric. The unexpected change in chords will draw attention to the words.

For example: *I Saw Her Standing There*

I	IV7	I	I7	V7	
C	F7	C	C7	G7	

I	IV	iv	I	V7	I
C	F	Fmin	C	G7	C

The Fmin does not belong to the key of C Major so it adds a nice touch of flavor to an otherwise ordinary chord progression.

Play through this sample progression first with the natural diatonic chords and then play the progression with the alterations:

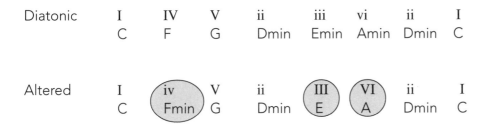

Diatonic	I	IV	V	ii	iii	vi	ii	I
	C	F	G	Dmin	Emin	Amin	Dmin	C

Altered	I	iv	V	ii	III	VI	ii	I
	C	Fmin	G	Dmin	E	A	Dmin	C

Minor Keys and Minor Key Substitutions

Here is a cool concept. You know how there are cities in the United States that have sister cities in other parts of the world? Well, every major key has a sister or brother as well and they are called relative minor keys. Count down three half steps from the root of a major scale. With that note now as the root, play through the scale. You are now playing the relative minor scale. Another way to think of it is this: the relative minor scale has the same notes as the major scale but starts and ends on the 6th degree of the major scale. So, in our example key, C Major, if we count down three half steps we find our new root note, A. So, the relative minor key of C Major is A Minor. The really impressive thing about this concept is that it is a very easy way to find chord substitutions.

Let's lay out our diatonic chords in C and compare them to its relative, A minor.

	I	ii	iii	IV	V	vi	vii°	I
Major:	C	Dmin	Emin	F	G	Amin	Bdim	C
	i	ii°	III	iv	v	VI	VII	i
Minor:	Amin	Bdim	C	Dmin	Emin	F	G	Amin

You can see that they use the exact same chords but that they fall in different positions. This makes their effect different. So, let's say, in the key of C, you were looking for an alternative to the IV chord. Look at the iv chord in the relative minor, A minor. It is a Dmin. Use that instead of your F Major chord. Generally speaking, you can substitute any chord using that method. Some will sound better than others. So, play around, have fun, and get used to seeing what works.

In the following examples you will find two straightforward progressions followed by ideas for substitutions. Play through them to hear the effect.

Straightforward:	I	IV	ii	vi	vii	vi	I
	C	F	Dmin	Amin	B°	Amin	C
Altered:	I	iv	ii	vi	♭vii	IV	I
	C	Dmin	B°	Amin	B♭°	F	C

Straightforward:	I	iii	ii	iii	vi
	C	Emin	Dmin	Emin	Amin
Altered:	i	♭iii	ii	III	VI
	Amin	E♭min	B°	C	F

○ = Circled chords are borrowed from the relative minor key.

☐ = Boxed chords show the technique of lowering a diatonic chord one half step (see page 19).

Putting a successful chord progression together takes practice. Let your ear and experience guide you.

Exercise

Play Chord Poker: 1) On index cards, write down the names of the diatonic chords in any key and its relative minor. Shuffle them and pull out four cards. Put these chords together (including a I chord whether you draw one or not) to form a verse. Rearrange them and make a chorus. Trade in one card and make a bridge. 2) Pull four new cards and make a progression in at least three different orders.

Melody

A melody, or tune, is the part of the song that gets sung. It is a series of notes that are strung together whose main purpose is to carry the lyric. It is not a clever chord progression, a cool guitar riff or a funky rhythm. A well written melody appears natural, as if the notes flow easily from one to the other. It is easy to sing and is simple and easy to remember. A melody can be broken down into several parts, which are often just repeating patterns (there's that pattern thing again!). These parts are called phrases. A phrase can be a few notes long or a dozen notes long. By stringing together phrases that have a pattern in common you are making it easier for the listener to remember the melody.

When writing a melody, it is helpful to keep a few things in mind:

1. *Range* - the average singer has a range of one to one and a half octaves. You will need to keep your melody within those boundaries. (Remember, an octave is the distance between two notes with the same name.) It is easy to cover the length of several octaves while playing a melody on an instrument. Be certain to sing along to make sure you are writing something that can be sung.

2. *Simplicity* - keeping the melody simple makes it easy to remember and sing. A shorter phrase as opposed to a longer phrase, like one that might be used in a guitar solo, is better. A good rule of thumb is that the phrase is the right length when you need to take a breath. Also, make sure the intervals (the distance between the notes) are not too wide or awkward to the ear.

3. *Singability* - sing your melody. It should sound as natural as speaking. After all, music is communication. When we speak, we take natural pauses to breathe or to emphasize a point. When sung, a melody needs exactly the same thing: places to breathe. It also should follow the natural syllables and accents of the words. This will automatically separate your melody line into groups of notes, or patterns, that the listener can easily identify.

Let's look at some examples:

Here is a phrase that is a good length and one that is too long:

Here is a singable phrase and a totally unsingable phrase:

Melodic and Rhythmic Motives

Very often, songwriters will create a melody by repeating a small melodic or rhythmic idea, known as a *motive*, over and over. The following songs are good examples of this:

Clementine (Traditional)

The Wedding March (Mendelsohn)

As with all parts of a song, the melody should contain a certain amount of continuity and repeating patterns. It should also have variety within and between the different sections (verse, chorus and bridge).

Where does the melody come from? Sometimes it comes from thin air, but more often than not it grows out of the chords that you have chosen for your progression. Simply, the notes of the melody will be notes that are contained in the chords, or the notes that move from one chord to another.

Let's look at it this way. If our song is in the key of C, we know that there are eight notes that make up the C Major scale. All of those notes can be used for our melody and the ones that will sound the best are the notes that make up the chords we are using. The notes in between those chords are called *passing tones*. We use them to get us from one chord to another. The easiest way to find a melody is to sing along with your chord progression. Look at the following progression and basic melody. Try substituting a melody of your own.

Be sure not to let all these "shoulds" and "should nots" get in the way of your writing. Obviously, you want to write something because it feels and sounds good to you and not because you are following the rules. It is keeping these things in mind when you are learning the process that will make them second nature to you.

Exercise

Over a chord progression, make a melody with two notes, then three notes, then four notes. Start with longer phrases. As you add more notes, make shorter phrases.

What Is Rhythm?

Rhythm is the element that holds your song together. If you tap your foot to a song, you are following its rhythm or beat. Rhythm can be felt in the lyrics as well as in the music. Every rhythm has its own texture and makes you feel a certain way. The rhythm of the song can determine its style. Dance tunes have a very strong pulse. Imagine being in a club and listening to the DJ spin records. The strong driving pulse of the bass and drums going 1-2-3-4, over and over again, makes you want to get up on the dance floor and move. This is the basis of rhythm.

Stevie Wonder
Few understand rhythm better than consummate songwriter, Stevie Wonder.

1 - 2 - 3 - 4 - 1 - 2 - 3 - 4...........

Rhythm carries the song forward.

Rhythms help determine the kind of feel or groove the song has (we'll talk about groove next). Rock and pop songs have a strong accent, or emphasis, on beats two and four:

1 - **2** - 3 - **4**

Jazz tunes frequently use what is called *swing*, where the *downbeats* (numbered parts of the beats) are held a little longer than the *upbeats* ("ands").

1...　and　2...　and　3...　and　4...　and

Your job is to place your song in the rhythmic setting that will work the best. Play around with the song's *tempo* (speed) to see what feels right.

Exercise

Pick three songs that have rhythms or beats that you like. Write a chord progression and put it to the rhythm of those three different songs.

In the Groove

The phrase "in the groove" comes from the image of a phonograph needle lining up in the groove of an LP. Rhythm is the key to the "feel" or "groove" of your song. It is the part of the song that makes you want to clap your hands or dance. A strong groove is absolutely essential for a dance tune of any kind. A groove is made up of the interplay between the musical parts of a song. *You Really Got Me* by the Kinks, *Hello, I Love You* by The Doors, *Satisfaction* by the Rolling Stones and *Get Up, Stand Up* by Bob Marley are all examples of songs that are built around a very strong groove and a memorable guitar riff. You can tell when a band is "in the groove" when all its members are playing together, listening to each other, locked into a solid rhythm.

Fine Tuning

As you progress through the writing of your song, you will feel the need to make adjustments. This is the fine tuning that was mentioned earlier. It is important to let yourself get far enough along in the process of hammering out ideas before you begin to edit and change things. Give yourself a chance to get all the good stuff on paper. Give it a chance to live and breathe on its own. Look at the pieces in relation to each other to see if they work together. Perhaps you need to change the melody a bit to highlight an important part of the lyric, or maybe the chord changes need to move a bit slower through a particular section to accommodate a particularly nice phrase in the melody. Sometimes you will find that things just don't seem to work at all and maybe a change in tempo will help pull it all together.

If you find yourself getting stuck with one part, move on to another or just put the whole thing away for awhile. Very often things just need to gel on their own. By allowing it to rest, you are giving your subconscious a chance to work for you.

PHOTO • DAVID SEELIG\COURTESY OF STARFILES, INC.

Tracy Chapman
A one time street performer, Tracy Chapman has become one of today's most influential songwriters.

Chord Charts

Just like a writer or a poet, the songwriter needs to be able to write down their words and musical ideas. How many times have you come up with an idea and neglected to put it down on paper because you were too lazy or just didn't know how to? Using a tape recorder is a great way to help you remember things and work out ideas. Eventually, you will have to write it all down. There are several ways to do this and all of them are easy. Let's start with easy way number one: the chord chart.

There are two kinds of chord charts. In its simplest form, the chord chart consists of lyrics and the chords that go with them. Write out the words and leave a space or two between each line. Then write the chord names above the words they go with. Write the title of the song at the top of the page in the center, and put your name along with a copyright symbol at the right hand margin (more about copyrights later on page 46). Look at the following example:

```
                    Barnyard Baby
                 ©1996 Josey O'McDonald

          C
          Tell me you won't go

          G
          As you drag me through the snow,

          Dmin              F        G
          Time and distance seem to disappear.

          C
          You've done your best, I know,

                  G
          As the rooster starts to crow.

          F             G            C
          Lord, I love you, oh, my darlin' dear.
```

Simple, eh? You could also mark the verses and choruses on the left side to make it easier for someone to follow when you say, "OK, Pat, take it from the second chorus..."

Verse: Lyrics.......

            Lyrics.....

Chorus: Lyrics.......

26

The second kind of chord chart uses a bit of standard notation along with the chord names. The slash marks serve to mark the beats in each measure without having to notate the melody. Fill in chord names where they fall in each measure, as you did in the previous chart. You can put in the words or leave them out. Keep the title and your name and copyright information.

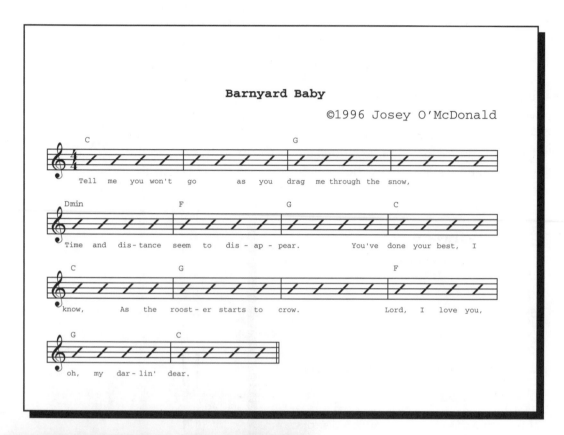

Barnyard Baby

©1996 Josey O'McDonald

C   G

Tell me you won't go   as you drag me through the snow,

Dmin   F   G   C

Time and dis-tance seem to dis-ap-pear.   You've done your best, I

C   G   F

know,   As the roost-er starts to crow.   Lord, I love you,

G   C

oh, my dar-lin' dear.

Mary-Chapin Carpenter
A great storyteller, Mary Chapin-Carpenter blends the best of contemporary folk and country.

Reading and Writing Lead Sheets

Lead sheets are a common method for notating songs. They use a combination of the chord chart and slash notation to give a pretty complete picture of what a song is all about. Lead sheets are especially helpful if there is a riff, or musical hook, which is important to the sound and feel of the song. It is also the easiest way to convey exactly how your song should sound to other musicians. All you need to do is to use the format for slash notation and write in the melody. Granted, that will take some practice, but the concept is an easy one.

Barnyard Baby

©1996 Josey O'McDonald

Tell me you won't go as you drag me through the snow,

Time and dis-tance seem to dis-ap-pear. You've done your best, I

know, as the roost-er starts to crow. Lord, I love you,

oh, my dar-lin' dear.

Chapter 3

PHOTO • CHUCK PULINCOURTESY OF STARFILES, INC.

John Hiatt
John Hiatt has written songs for some of the most popular artists on the scene today, such as Bonnie Raitt, Iggy Pop and Jeff Healey.

The lyrics are the words of the song. There are many aspects to consider in writing successful lyrics. Along with the music, they should literally sing the message that the writer wishes to share with the listener. A strong lyric has emotion, clear imagery and should fit the feel and rhythm of the music. The beat of the words and the beat of the music accompanying those words should be woven together smoothly. The language should be clear and simple. The message should be easily understood without relying on clichés.

An idea for a song can come from many different sources. Many talented writers wait for inspiration to begin. This is a fine way to write and you can sit down with that intention. To write *only* in this way would be a grave error if you wish to reach your potential. A runner who has the ability to run a four minute mile but doesn't train will never finish the race. Great lyrics are written by songwriters who practice and work toward those moments of inspiration. They are ready when lightning strikes. Many songwriters keep a notebook where they collect ideas, lines and images. Make writing a regular practice. When you are not writing, be sure you are listening. Reading, listening to people's conversations, watching T.V. or going to the movies may give you ideas for a great song. Listening to other songwriters can be inspiring and spark your creativity. A great title can sometimes suggest the rest of a lyric.

Keep your eyes and ears open. Your own life experiences are often a great place to begin. Your life is interesting and unique. Often, the most personal songs are the ones that touch the most people. As Woody Guthrie said, "Write what you know."

Here are some examples of songs with really great lyrics to inspire you:

TITLE	ARTIST	TITLE	ARTIST
This Old Shirt	Mary-Chapin Carpenter	*Hotel California*	Don Henley
Get Here	Brenda Russell	*The Weight*	Robbie Robertson
Sounds of Silence	Paul Simon	*I Don't Know Why*	Shawn Colvin
The Race Is On	George Jones	*Trouble in the Fields*	Nanci Griffith
Yesterday	Paul McCartney	*Kiss From a Rose*	Seal

Titles

The title is often the first or last line of a chorus or verse. The title should be easily remembered and provide the listener with easy access to your song. It can be one or more words. The title is often the hook or main idea of the song. The title is usually a description of what the song is really about. Examples of this would include *Tears in Heaven* by Eric Clapton, *Get on Your Feet* by Miami Sound Machine, *The Road is My Middle Name* by Bonnie Raitt or *Passionate Kisses* by Lucinda Williams.

> *Exercise*
> Write twenty-five new titles for songs that are four words or less.

Imagery

A solid lyric evokes responses from the listener's senses. They should be able to feel, see and smell whatever is going on in the song. A strong lyric will flood the listener with their own memories and experiences. The secret is to paint pictures with words that take the listener where you want them to go. Remember: show, don't tell. *Love at the Five and Dime* by Nanci Griffith or *When Haley Came to Jackson* by Mary-Chapin Carpenter are good examples of this technique.

> *Exercise*
> Pick a very descriptive song that you like. Replace those images with other images. Like "Joe thought he was cool, with a biker jacket and a long, tall brew," with "Joe was a fool in his hospital bed, wishing he hadn't let it all go to his head." Or, take a color, a street and an article of clothing and write a verse around them.

Universal Themes

If you want your songs to appeal to as many people as possible then you need to address topics that everybody can relate to. Universal themes cover the topics that everybody has in common; love, birth, death, taxes—any subject common to the human experience. The trick is to concentrate on your own life and the lives of those around you and then broaden the personal into the universal. You connect the individual experience to these universal subjects. If this is done correctly, the listener will be thinking about their own life and not yours. Examples of this would be *You Don't Have to Say You're Sorry* by Patti Austin or *Leaving on a Jet Plane* by Paul Stookey.

> *Exercise*
> Take a major happening in your life, such as your high school graduation, prom night or your first kiss. Describe it in detail. Then tell the story as if it had happened to someone else.

Be Specific

A song that generalizes too much won't have anything in it that people can be excited about or moved by. If there are not any details, there won't be enough information to make it real. Trust the listener to hear the story within the story. If you have an experience that is too personal, or painful, you can use it by putting it into a fictional context. Change the names to protect the innocent, and especially the guilty. It doesn't matter if the story is real or not, as long as the emotions ring true. The audience will sense the truth within it. Many writers change tense; go from the past to the present, or the present to the future. For example, let's say you write a song about your first love. The first thing to do would be to make a list of everything you can think of, in detail, about your own experience. Then try to tell the story from someone else's perspective. For examples listen to *Every Little Thing She Does Is Magic* by Sting or *I Married Her Because She Looks Like You* by Lyle Lovett.

Exercise

Take a song like *Eleanor Rigby* by Lennon and McCartney. It is chock full of description and detail. Write about it and get as general and mundane as you can. For instance, you could say that the first verse is about a woman who is all by herself. By doing this it will be easy to see the difference between lots of detail and no detail at all.

Lyrics and Rhythm

Every language has an inherent rhythm—the beat of the words. Even different accents can create a different pattern of speech. It is easy to hear the rhythm of a language when it is not your own, because you are not listening to the meaning of the words. An experienced writer can hear the rhythm of the words within the music. Consider the word "symphony." It has three beats, with the accent on the first beat. The word "watermelon" has four beats, "world" has only one. Rap and hip hop artists are extremely gifted at working with the rhythm of words and creating patterns. Examples of this would be many songs by Queen Latifah, Boys II Men, or En Vogue.

Exercise

Take popular television theme songs or nursery rhymes and speak them in a rap style, feeling the accents in the appropriate places.

To Rhyme or Not to Rhyme

Rhyme is an excellent way to develop a sense of pattern in a song. There is a comfort in the expectation that the next line will rhyme. The two basic kinds of rhymes are hard rhymes and soft rhymes. A hard rhyme is like a line in a nursery rhyme. Like "lime" and "rhyme," "time" and "crime." A soft rhyme has the same vowel sound, but may start or end differently: "I don't mind that it doesn't exactly rhyme." "Mind" and "rhyme" are soft rhymes. Sometimes a hard rhyme can be a little heavy handed: "When I went to the store,

and opened the door, a pail of water fell down on the floor." A soft rhyme may still tighten the song form without creating a "singsong" feel. The song's format helps determine the rhyme scheme (patterns of rhymes) within a section of the song.
For example, take this nursery rhyme:

Twinkle twinkle little star
How I wonder what you are
Up above the world so high
Like a diamond in the sky
Twinkle twinkle little star
How I wonder what you are

Common Rhyme Schemes

Poets and songwriters use a letter shorthand that is similar to the verse/chorus shorthand that we've already discussed on page 8. For example, the rhyme scheme for *Twinkle, Twinkle Little Star* is A-A-B-B-A-A.

Twinkle twinkle little <u>star</u>	A
How I wonder what you <u>are</u>	A
Up above the world so <u>high</u>	B
Like a diamond in the <u>sky</u>	B
Twinkle twinkle little <u>star</u>	A
How I wonder what you <u>are</u>	A

If we had written the second verse to this classic, we would have rhymed the last word in each of the first two lines together (A), rhyme the third and fourth lines together (B), and the last two lines would rhyme with the first two (A). This second verse is from its parody in <u>Alice in Wonderland</u> by Lewis Carol:

Twinkle twinkle little bat	A
How I wonder what you're at	A
Up above the world you fly	B
Like a tea tray in the sky	B
Twinkle twinkle little bat	A
How I wonder what you're at	A

Even if the second verse's first two lines don't rhyme with the first verse's, it still works as long as they rhyme with each other. You are imitating the pattern.

Exercises
- Write a verse that has the rhyme scheme A-A-A-A. The last word of each phrase must rhyme with sour.
- Write a verse or chorus that has this rhyme scheme: A-B-A-B. The words in the first two lines must rhyme with sing and run.
- Write a verse or chorus with the following rhyme schemes: A-A-A-B, A-B-B-A and A-B-C-A.
- Using a dictionary, pick five words at random and use two of them to write a verse or chorus. Use any rhyme scheme mentioned above.

Which Comes First?

So, what comes first...the music or the lyrics? There is no simple answer to this question. It depends on the songwriter. A versatile songwriter is like a major league pitcher. The pitcher may have gotten into the majors because of his great fast-ball, but he has to be able to throw many different pitches to really win ball games. You may be a lyric oriented person. So, lyrics first may be your primary inspiration. Or, you may be an excellent player with unlimited musical riffs. It doesn't matter which area is your strength. Start with your strengths but expand your horizons. Try to write from all possible angles. You may find that each approach brings out different aspects of your writing. The broader your skill base, the more interesting your songs will be, and the better your chances are of becoming a first class songwriter.

Lyrics First

Let's say you have a story, a line or a hook you want to develop into a song. You can start by deciding what style the music should be to match the mood of your lyrical idea. Is the feel of the lyric somber or upbeat, fast or slow? Listen to the inherent rhythm of the words and try and match the beat of the lyric to the musical rhythms. If it is a very complicated story or idea, use a less complicated musical background so that the audience can concentrate on the lyric. A basic lyric idea may sit well in a more developed musical pattern. A good rule of thumb is if you can understand what's going on after the first hearing, you are probably in the ballpark. Have a friend listen to what you've got until you develop your own musical intuition. If you have a few lines or a complete lyric, try different musical styles and speeds until something clicks. It doesn't matter which comes first, the music or the lyrics, as long as it sounds like one complete unit when you're done.

Music First

Another way to write is to start with a chord progression or pattern. You can put the music on a cassette and listen to it over and over. What images or pictures does the music conjure up for you? As soon as you get a word or image, try to put it in the context of the music. One word may suggest the next phrase and you will be off and running. The beat of the chord progression can be altered. Try different drum patterns underneath the chords. Try different tempos. When you get something you like, listen to the beat and experiment with different word combinations. You can even get out the dictionary and write down words you like without worrying about how you are going to use them. Play around with the words and the chords. Let your subconscious have a chance to experiment. Sometimes the best songs come from just goofing around.

Words and Music Simultaneously

Some songwriters have the experience of having the music and lyrics come to them at the same time. Usually this comes after a lot of practice. If you work at developing your writing skills, you will be more likely to write a song when inspiration strikes. Many writers talk about the song that "just came to them." The song may take minutes to write. On page 34 are suggestions for what is called "writing practice." Doing exercises like these will make it more likely that this kind of spontaneous writing will happen.

A Word About Rewriting

Recycling is an important and useful tool for the songwriter. Sometimes you will get lots of ideas all together that really belong in different songs. Remember that we are working with pieces of a puzzle. The creative process is very organic. It comes out like it comes out, in no particular order. And very rarely will it come out exactly the way it should. It is your job to be able to let yourself come up with ideas and then be able to put them all together in the way that works best for the song; to make adjustments and compromises. You could call this "keeping the creator and the editor separate."

For example, a great chorus and great verse that don't seem to work together may not be parts of the same song. Save one or the other and use it later. There is no shame in this; it is very resourceful. By the same token, great chord progressions or lyrics that came from your earlier efforts are worth taking second looks at. Reflection, and years, can give you new insights on how to rewrite and improve. It is often well worth the effort. Remember that every song you write will not be your best, but every song you write will be an opportunity for you to learn more about yourself and your craft.

Learning by Listening

One of the best schools for songwriting is in your CD collection. There's no reason to reinvent the wheel. Listen to your favorite writers. Try and learn what they did, and how they did it. A good way to learn is to analyze the structure, rhyme scheme and chord patterns of some of your favorite songs. Take a chord progression from a classic fifties rock song, like I-vi-IV-V, and try to write a song with that kind of feel.

Ask yourself these kinds of questions:

1. What were the major themes of that style and what connections can you draw from your own life?
2. If the songs are about cruising through town in a great car, what is cruising like in your town on Saturday night?
3. What type of car would you drive?
4. Where do you go to dance or get a bite to eat?

You can learn by imitating what's happened before. When you have mastered the themes associated with each style, why not try writing about something that usually isn't discussed in that style, like a divorce song in a hard rock style, or a song about a perfect picnic in a speed metal style. Maybe a rap song about tractors. Have fun and experiment.

Generating Ideas

While it's all well and good to wait around for inspiration to strike, there are lots of ways to practice writing songs. The trick is being able to write whether the Great Spirit is around at the time or not. So, how about a list of some ways to help stimulate the creative spark?

1. Make a list of interesting titles. Try to write twenty titles. Pick one and try writing a complete lyric for it. If that doesn't work, try another title.

2. Look through a dictionary or thesaurus and write down twenty words you like. See if you can use any of them together to get a good idea going.

3. Go sit in a busy park or mall and just write what you see for twenty minutes. Try turning some of these events into a story idea for a song.

4. Sit down for five minutes and write about what is going on outside of your window. Even descriptions of the scenery may end up being useful when you need to create a scene in a song.

5. Pick five emotions and write a paragraph on each one.

6. Make up a story about someone you see in the grocery store. Use your imagination; it will become more effective and limber if you exercise it.

7. Take a standard twelve-bar blues progression and write a song in a different style, like bluegrass perhaps. A twelve-bar blues follows the basic **I-IV-V** progression. In the key of C, it goes like this:

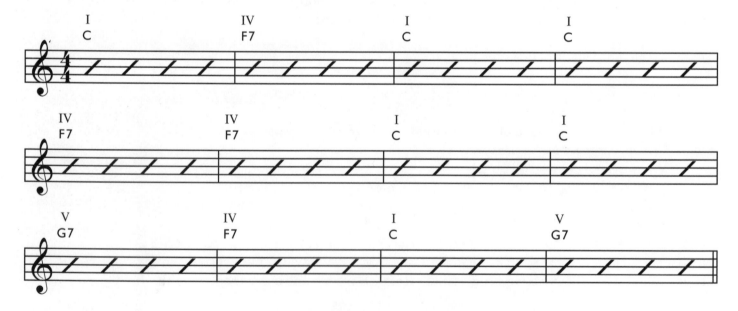

8. Try writing a song on one instrument and playing it on another. A song you've been fooling around with on guitar may blossom on piano.

9. Take a movie plot or short story and try to tell it in song form.

10. Keep a notebook, file or a box where you write down or store ideas as you get them. Record musical ideas on tape. When you sit down to write, just pick an idea out of your collection and go with it. Don't throw your ideas away—you may use them later.

Bob Dylan
Bob Dylan's lyrics made him the spokesperson for a generation.

PHOTO • MARK HARLAN/COURTESY OF STARFILES, INC.

Common Song Titles

There are lots of different kinds of songs you can write. Fast, slow, a dance tune, a rockabilly tune, a chicken pickin' thing. It can be confusing to know exactly how to go about doing that. Listen, listen, listen. A successful songwriter is one who is not limited to writing in any particular way. Writing in different styles forces you to grow and stretch your abilities as a musician. Knowing what you like, and doing a lot of listening and analyzing, are the first steps towards being versatile as a writer. When attempting to write in a style you are unaccustomed to:

1. Listen to and analyze the style you want to write in.

2. Determine what kinds of chord progressions are commonly used.

3. Figure out what the groove is like.

4. Think about what kinds of stories are generally told.

You can write songs in an endless number of styles, especially with world music making its way into contemporary song styles. There are all kinds of hybrids and lots of cultural mixing. The possibilities are endless.

As a place to start, here's a list of the more commonly used styles and a few artists who represent them. This book has given you the tools you need to analyze and interpret just about any song you hear. So, listen to as many of them as you can and learn!

Folk	Pete or Peggy Seeger, Peter, Paul and Mary
Folk/Rock	Jackson Brown, Crosby, Stills, Nash and Young
Acoustic or Electric Blues	Muddy Waters, Robert Johnson
Rhythm and Blues	James Brown, The Isley Brothers
Contemporary Folk/Acoustic	Shawn Colvin, David Wilcox, Nanci Griffith
Bluegrass	Allison Kraus, Ralph Stanley, Tony Rice
Rockabilly	Eddie Cochran, Gene Vincent
50's, 60's, 70's Rock	Bill Haley, Chuck Berry, Rolling Stones, The Doors
Hard Rock	Led Zeppelin, AC/DC
Heavy Metal	Metallica, Black Sabbath
Country	Dolly Parton, Willie Nelson, Bob Wills, Hank Williams, Sr.
Swing	Duke Ellington, Glenn Miller, Count Basie
Pop	The Beatles, Stevie Wonder, Barry Gordy,
Soul	Marvin Gaye, Otis Redding
Gospel	Mahalia Jackson, The Wynans
Punk	Sex Pistols, The Clash
Alternative	Green Day, Pearl Jam, Nirvana, Smashing Pumpkins
New Wave	Blondie, The Pretenders
Broadway/Show Music	George Gershwin, Rodgers and Hammerstein, Marvin Hamlish
Reggae	Bob Marley, Black Uhuru, Peter Tosh
Latin	Gloria Estefan, Selena
Jazz	Michael Franks, Bobby McFerrin, Alberta Hunter

Protecting Your Songs—To Copyright or Not to Copyright

Even if all the songs you write never find their way into the commercial marketplace, more and more people are interested in getting their songs commercially recorded. Being aware of your rights and responsibilities as a writer will help protect you and your material.

Legally, the moment you write a song, you own it. To establish this ownership all you need do is mark all your lead sheets, lyrics and tapes with this information: © [Year], [Your name].

The best way to insure that you will be able to prove a song is yours is to register it with the copyright office in Washington, DC. For a fee of $20 you can register one or more songs. Call the copyright office to request the proper forms (form PA for written music or a lead sheet and lyrics or form SR for a sound recording [tape or CD]). The number is:

(202) 707-9100

Or, write:

United States Copyright Office
Library of Congress
Washington, DC., 20559

If you have a fax machine you can have the forms faxed to you by calling (202) 707-2600. Or, if you are on the Internet you can download forms to your computer and print them out yourself. Go to the Library of Congress at this address: http://lcweb.loc.gov and select the copyright link. You can also use http://lcweb.loc.gov/copyright to go directly to the Copyright Office home page.

Once you receive the forms, fill them out and send them to the copyright office with your money. Include a cassette with all your songs recorded on it (a simple hum and strum is fine) with lyric sheets. You can send lead sheets as well. It is not necessary to send both.

You can copyright one song at time, but if you are not made of money, it is more economical to copyright several songs at one time. On the forms that you will be filling out, mark that you are copyrighting a collection of songs and then give the collection a name like, Jane Doe's Greatest Hits. You can copyright all of those for a one time fee.

Now lets say that Anita Baker or Green Day hears one of those songs being sung in a club and they want to record it. Remember that one song's copyright is part of the collection. The smart thing to do would be to take that one song and copyright it again, this time by itself. That way you will not be opening yourself up for potential confusion over the ownership of any of your other material.

Appendix A

Keyboard Diagrams

The following diagrams show the basic I-IV-V progression on the keyboard in several different keys. Each chord gets played in the same octave. The numbers along the bottom of the keys represent the fingers of your right hand (1 is the thumb, 2 your index, 3 your middle finger and so on).

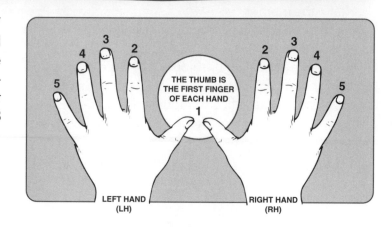

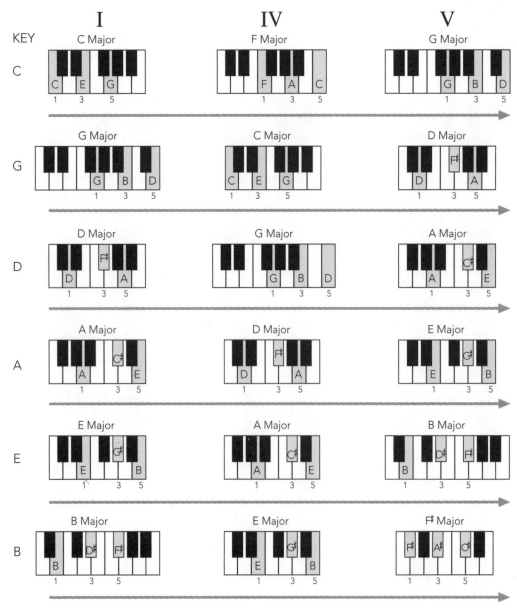

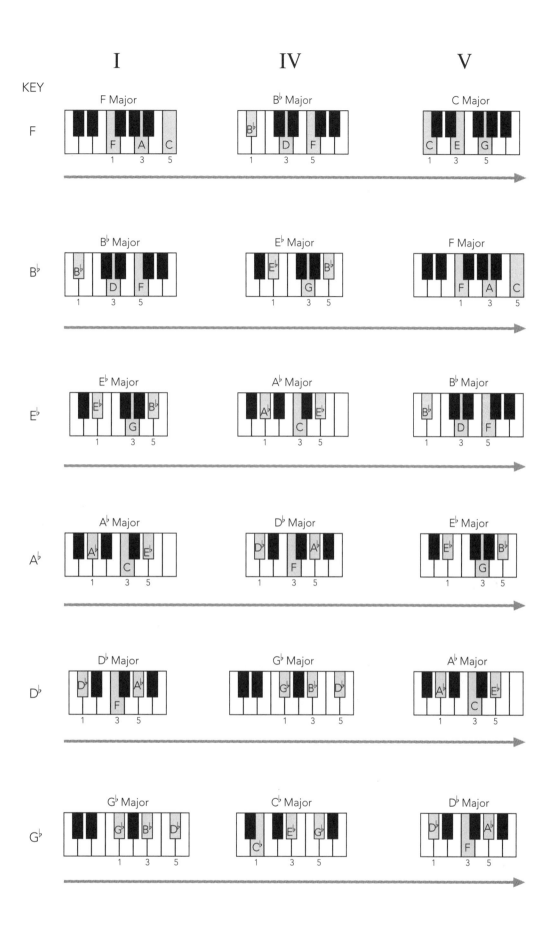

Here are keyboard diagrams for the four types of 7th chords you have learned in this book. They are all shown with C roots. See page 16 for a full explanation of the 7th chord formulas, and try building these chords from all possible roots. If you read through the chord scales provided on pages 46 and 47, you will encounter all of these in all the keys.

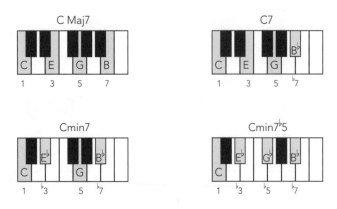

Billy Joel
Billy Joel is a master
of the pop song
format

Guitar Chords

Chord frames show the top portion of the guitar neck. The vertical lines are the strings and the horizontal lines are the frets. The numbers across the top are the left hand fingerings (1 is your index finger, 2 is your middle finger, 3 is your ring finger and 4 is your pinky). An "x" is an unplayed string and an "o" is an open string. When one finger plays more than one string (a *barre* chord) it is shown with a curve crossing all the strings covered by that finger. The Roman numeral to the right of the chord box guides you to the correct fret. See page 14 for a quick review of Roman numerals.

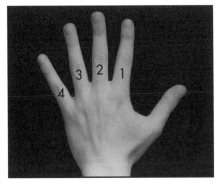

The fingers of the left hand are numbered.

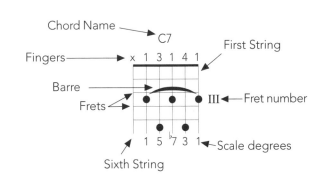

The following diagrams show chord boxes for the I-IV-V progression in several different keys.

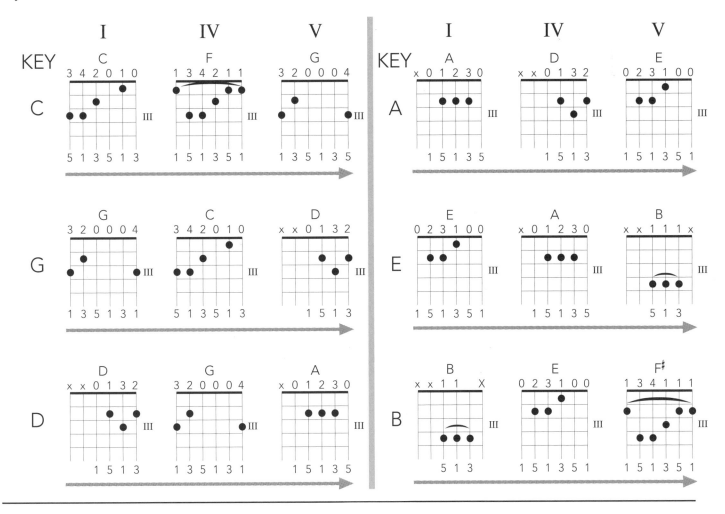

(Guitar Chords, continued)

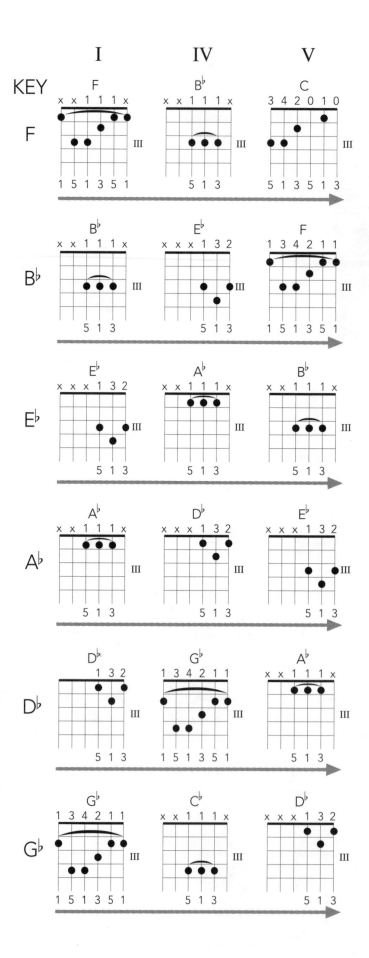

Moveable Chords

Since barre chords involve no open strings, it is possible to play them from any root. That is why we often refer to them as *moveable* chords. Any chord that does not require open strings can be a movable chord. You only need to know which note of the chord is the root and where the root is located on the neck of the guitar. For instance, the F chord shown as the I chord in the key of F on page 42 can become a G chord if you play it on the 3rd fret. The note on the 6th string of that chord form is the root, and the note G is on the 3rd fret.

The two most common types of moveable chords are root ⑥ chords, with the root on the 6th string, and root ⑤ chords, with the root on the 5th string. The chart on the right shows the moveable chord forms for the basic chord types used in this book. Knowing these will allow you to write songs in any key.

The guitar diagrams on page 44 will help you learn the names of the notes on the 6th and 5th strings, so that you can find any root easily.

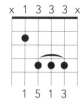

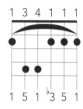

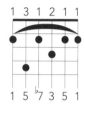

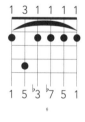

⑥= 6th string. A circled number indicates a string.

Notes on the 5th and 6th Strings

Root ⑤ Names

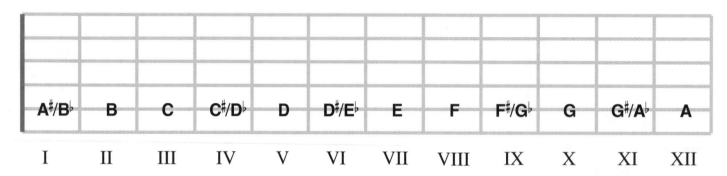

Root ⑥ Names

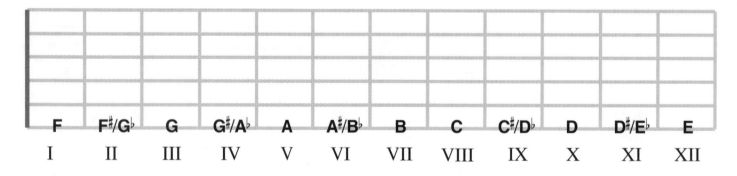

Appendix B

Suggested Reading and Resource Materials

Once you have mastered the basics of songwriting you may be in the market for some other resource materials. There are lots of books and magazines out there with valuable information. Many are included here; some about songwriting, others about the creative process. Always listen and allow yourself to grow. It is the only way to become the songwriter you wish to be. Good luck!

A Musician's Guide to Publicity and Promotion (video), Diane Rapaport
     Workshop Arts, Litchfield, CT

Listening Out Loud—Becoming a Composer, Elizabeth Swados
     Harper and Row, NY

Music and Imagination, Aaron Copland
     Harvard University Press, Cambridge, MA

Music Publishing: A Songwriter's Guide, Randy Doe
     Writer's Digest Books, Cinti, OH

Protecting Your Songs and Yourself: The Songwriter's Legal Guide, Kent Klavins
     Writer's Digest Books, Cinti, OH

Recording Industry Sourcebook, Ascona Communications

The Artist's Way—A Spiritual Path to Higher Creativity, Julia Cameron with Mark Bryan
     Tarcher/Putnam Books, New York

The Billboard Book of Songwriting, Pickow and Appleby
     Writer's Digest Books, Cinti, OH

This Business of Music, M. Krasilovky, Sidney Shemel
     Billboard Publications

The Craft and Business of Songwriting, John Braheny
     Writer's Digest Books, Cinti, OH

The Craft of Lyric Writing, Sheila Davis
     Writer's Digest Books, Cinti, OH

The Songwriter's Market
     Writer's Digest Books, Cinti, OH

Writing Down the Bones—Freeing the Writer Within, Natalie Goldberg
     Shambala Pub. Boston, MA

Wild Mind-Living the Writer's Life, Natalie Goldberg
     Bantam Books, New York

Appendix C

The charts on these pages show the 7th chords that belong in every major and minor key. When all the chords built on the notes of a scale are shown together in this manner, they are called a *chord scale*. Play through these on the keyboard (just read them as is, adding the root note in a lower octave in the left hand) or on the guitar (use the moveable chord forms discussed on pages 43 and 44). This will familiarize you with all of the keys, and make it easier for you to make creative chord choices in any key. Notice that the flats or sharps used to create the key are extracted and placed before the music just next to the clef. This is called a *key signature*. You should memorize the key signature for each key.

Major Keys

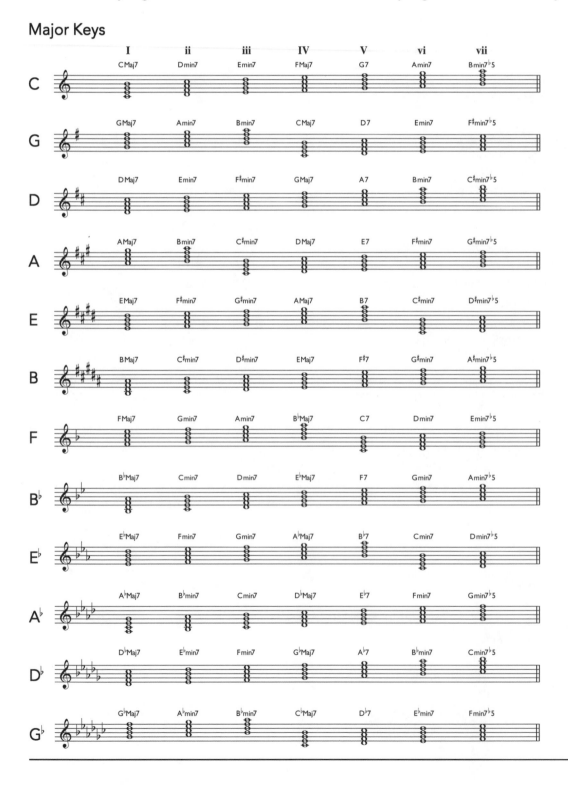

In a minor key, it is common to substitute a dominant 7 V chord for the minor 7 v chord that is diatonic to the key. For instance, in the key of A Minor, the diatonic v chord is Emin7. It is common, however, to use a non-diatonic V chord, which in this case is E7.

Minor Keys

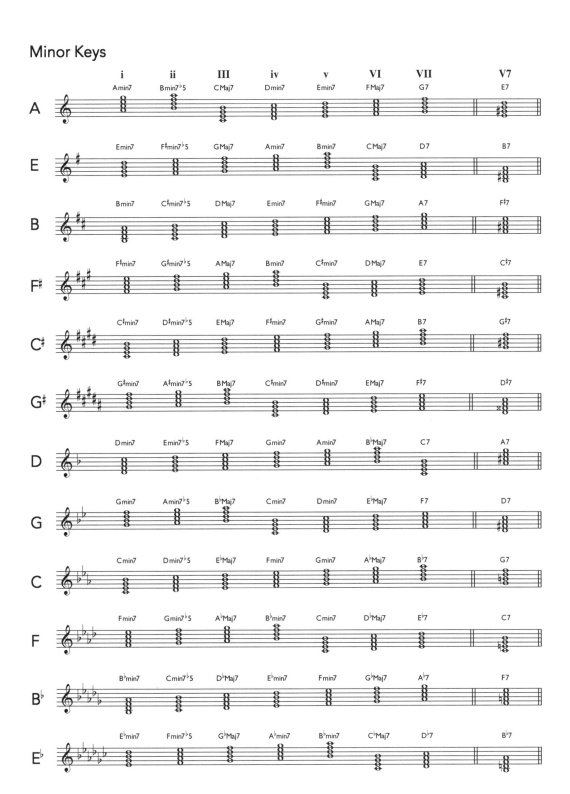

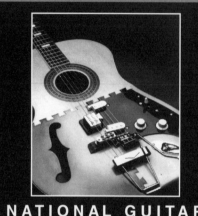